30 DAYS OF SITUATIONAL PRAYER

BY

WINNYE WILKS

Introduction

God has purposely created a season of quietness in my life and during this time it has allowed me to hear his voice regarding several areas in which I needed revelation. One is self-sacrifice. Not just giving up something during the Lenten season but recommitting myself to God and his works. Prayer is something that I know can work in anyone's life because it has worked in mine. Those things I have prayed about consistently have been revealed, not always to my desire, but sometimes the resolution God desired for me. When I reflect on my most consistent prayer, it was for the health and longevity of my parents, which God saw fit to manifest.

Prayer and meditation are an essential part of our faith journey. Consistent prayer regarding those things that challenge us daily can prove to be powerful enough to affect real and sustainable change. The following is a collection of simple prayers that, when done daily, can have a remarkable impact on your life. Prayers do not have to be long to be meaningful. It is the consistency in our prayer life that can move mountains. I encourage you to engage in a 30-day regimen of prayer regarding some of the topics highlighted in this prayer guide and journal your outcomes at the end of each 30-day period. This methodology has worked for me, and I pray that it works in your life.

I am thankful for the turning down of the noise in my life because it has allowed me to honor God with this small project that I hope will have great impact in the life of everyone who leverages it.

Situations that need constant prayer

Jealousy

"Jealousy makes a man rage; he'll show no mercy on his day of revenge."

- Proverbs 6:34

Day 1

God, overcome my spirit of jealousy, with a sense of knowing that what he's done for others he can also do for me.

Day 2

Heavenly Father, please remove the thorns from my heart and wash it with love.

Day 3

Father God, help me to know that jealousy and envy only block my future blessings, order my steps.

Day 4

Lord, remove the barrier of jealousy and let your blessings rush in like a mighty flood.

Day 5

God, jealousy is like a festering wound that can only be closed by the ointment of love and salvation, so provide me with the balm.

Day 6

God, give others contentment regarding the blessings you have already bestowed upon them.

Day 7

Lord, help us all to rejoice in the success of others and know that it is your works that have provided this success.

Day 8

Heavenly Father, allow gratefulness to reside where envy once did.

Day 9

Father, help me to be a cheerleader for others and rejoice in their success.

Day 10

God, you have unique blessings only designed for me.

Day 11

God, allow my heart to rejoice for others like angelic voices singing your praise.

Day 12

Lord, allow me to focus on my abundant blessings and not covet those of others.

Day 13

God, let your spirit of compassion dwell in me.

Day 14

Father, let me walk on the path of love and encouragement daily.

Day 15

God, I know love is blind, but envy is targeted and specific, so let love rule.

Day 16

God almighty, grant me the wisdom to respond to jealousy through loving acts of kindness.

Day 17

Lord, teach me to love those who lash out at me due to jealousy.

Day 18

God, give me contentment regarding the blessings I have already received.

Day 19

Lord, build a hedge of protection around me and shield me from the destructive nature of jealousy.

Day 20

Heavenly Father, help me to uplift others at every turn.

Day 21

Father God, replace envy with a spirit of generosity and encouragement.

Day 22

God, may my heart be a cup of generosity and love that overflows for others.

Day 23

Lord, cultivate a garden of gratitude that can harvest in all situations.

Day 24

Lord, give me the strength and independence to not walk in the shadow of jealousy.

Day 25

Father, let positivity flow from my lips at every opportunity.

Day 26

Almighty God, let seeds of gratefulness be the only fruits that harvest in my garden.

Day 27

God, equip me with the breastplate of humility and shield me from jealousy.

Day 28

God, cut down the roots of jealousy so that its spirit cannot flourish.

Day 29

Lord, light my path with a spirit of love that shines so bright it rebukes the darkness of jealousy.

Day 30

God, I desire peace and success for everyone at all times.

LESSONS FROM YOUR 30 DAY JOURNEY

(document your learnings from your 30 days of situational prayer)

Lies

"Do not let any unwholesome talk come out of your mouth, but only what is helpful for building others up according to their needs, that it may benefit those who listen "

-Ephesians 4:29

Day 1

God, grant me the strength to embrace truth and rebuke lies.

Day 2

Lord, let not the lying tongue destroy the temple of truth.

Day 3

God, let truth overshadow the dwelling place of lies.

Day 4

Father God, give me the discernment to know the difference between truth and lies.

Day 5

Heavenly Father, let the light of truth drive out the darkness of lies.

Day 6

God, teach your people that all lies, great or small, are contrary to your will and word.

Day 7

Lord, shield me from the temptation of lies and deceit.

Day 8

God, give me a sword so sharp that it can strike down lies with your truth.

Day 9

Father, make me a beacon of truth and a warrior against lies.

Day 10

Lord, allow me to carry the banner of truth and advocate for its existence.

Day 11

God, prevent me from being a seeker of gossip and slander.

Day 12

Father, may I find freedom in truth and rebuke the bondage of lies.

Day13

Lord, let my words reflect the genuineness of my heart.

Day 14

God, shield me with armor that deflects all lies.

Day 15

Almighty God, let truth be the light in a forest of lies.

Day 16

Lord, let the truth be as beautiful as Lillies in the valley.

Day 17

God, let truth be the pathway and bridge to trust.

Day 18

Lord, help them to know that truth breeds loyalty.

Day 19

Father God, mend the hearts that have been broken by lies.

Day 20

Almighty God, let truthfulness be as pure gold and cherished as such.

Day 21

Lord, free me from my web of lies and cleanse me with the soothing spirit of truth.

Day 22

God, always allow me to carry the banner of truth and may it never be too heavy.

Day 23

Father God, may truth be a source of comfort to those who have been tattered by lies.

Day 24

God, make shinny those who have been tarnished by lies.

Day 25

Lord, let truth be my conscience and lies be my enemy.

Day 26

God, help others to see truth in me.

Day 27

Father, let tears and truth soften the tough veneer of lies.

Day 28

God, wash our tongues with the sweet savor of the truth.

Day 29

Lord, let the truth be as a sweet aroma in my nostrils.

Day 30

Father, let truth be the longest liver amongst lies.

LESSONS FROM YOUR 30 DAY JOURNEY

(document your learnings from your 30 days of situational prayer)

Discrimination

"But whoever hates his brother, is in the darkness, and walks in the darkness, and does not know where he is going, because the darkness has blinded his eyes. "

- 1 John 2:11

Day 1

God, heal their heart with love for all people.

Day 2

Lord, we are all uniquely designed by you. Let us love the differences.

Day 3

Father, help me to treat everyone with dignity and respect.

Day 4

Heavenly Father, help me to see the beauty in diversity, and the fruitfulness it brings.

Day 5

God, give me the conscience to think about how my actions affect others.

Day 6

Lord, create in me a spirit of love and kindness that overlooks others' differences and flaws.

Day 7

Father, grant me the strength to speak up against racism and discrimination.

Day 8

God, let me lead with a changed heart, and a fair hand.

Day 9

Father, help them to know we are all your children and equal in your eyes.

Day 10

God, help me to embrace the differences in others with a welcoming heart.

Day 11

Father God, may my judgement of others be cast into the sea and help me to see their goodness.

Day 12

God, let the differences in others help to improve my own inadequacies.

Day 13

Lord, give me the courage to breakdown stereotypical strongholds.

Day 14

Almighty God, open their eyes to hate and the limitations it creates, replace hate with love.

Day 15

Heavenly Father, help me avoid the closing walls of hate and the isolation it creates.

Day 16

Lord, the person who hates or discriminates will lead a cold and lonely life without the warmth that love provides. Change their heart.

Day 17

God, help me to uplift those who have been marginalized and serve as their advocate.

Day 18

Father, help me to be a champion of equality, justice, and understanding.

Day 19

Lord, give the act of inclusion the power to defeat discrimination.

Day 20

God, give leaders the voice and integrity to create a discrimination free environment within their organization.

Day 21

Almighty God, help me point out and uplift acts of inclusion.

Day 22

Lord, help me to build bridges between cultures and sexes to promote diversity.

Day 23

God, erase the divisions that discrimination creates, and unite us in love.

Day 24

Lord, empower us to dismantle discriminatory systems and structures.

Day 25

Father, grant us the grace to see beyond outward differences and appreciate the individuality that you created.

Day 26

Lord, break the chains of discrimination that bind our world.

Day 27

Father, inspire us to stand in solidarity with those who face discrimination.

Day 28

Father God, may empathy and compassion guide our interactions with others.

Day 29

Heavenly Father, grant us the humility to learn from diverse perspectives and experiences.

Day 30

Lord, grant us the courage to be agents of change, promoting equality.

LESSONS FROM YOUR 30 DAY JOURNEY

(document your learnings from your 30 days of situational prayer)

Adultery

"No temptation has overtaken you that is not common to man. God is faithful, and he will not let you be tempted beyond your ability, but with the temptation, he will also provide the way of escape, that you may be able to endure it".

-1 Corinthians 10:13.

Day 1

Lord, protect my heart from wandering.

Day 2

God, grant me the strength to honor my relational commitments.

Day 3

Father, forgive me for straying from righteousness and your word.

Day 4

Lord, lead me away from temptation's grasp.

Day 5

God, renew my love and covenant commitments daily.

Day 6

God, keep my eyes fixed on the blessing that you have provided.

Day 7

Lord, rid my mind of un-pure thoughts and temptations.

Day 8

God, guide me in paths of faithfulness and help me avoid tempestuous paths.

Day 9

Father, help me to not be the source of betrayal.

Day 10

Almighty God, may my actions honor my sacred vows.

Day 11

God, guard my heart against the impurity of temptation.

Day 12

Lord, grant me the wisdom to choose the path you would have me travel.

Day 13

Heavenly Father, help me restore the trust that has been broken by betrayal.

Day 14

Father God, strengthen me and close my wandering eyes.

Day 15

God, let love and fidelity reign in my relationships.

Day 16

Lord, keep me steadfast and accountable to my promises.

Day 17

God, help me to cherish the relational gift that you have blessed me with.

Day 18

Father God, help me to offer forgiveness and grace toward those who break their promises.

Day 19

Lord, help me resist those who seek to threaten my commitment.

Day 20

Father, help me to be enough for my chosen one and for them to always be enough for me.

Day 21

God, lead me down the path of righteousness.

Day 22

Father, put a hedge of protection around my relationship.

Day 23

Lord, wrap me in your cloak of devotion daily.

Day 24

Almighty God, strengthen my heart and love daily.

Day 25

Lord, let the beauty of my relationship never fade.

Day 26

Lord, help me to understand that lust is the trick of the enemy.

Day 27

God, help me to value the sanctity of marriage and know that it is your will and desire for us.

Day 28

Heavenly Father, help me seek forgiveness when I am wrong.

Day 29

God, renew my heart and commitment daily.

Day 30

 Father, help me to never measure my partner against the standards of others.

LESSONS FROM YOUR 30 DAY JOURNEY

(document your learnings from your 30 days of situational prayer)

Hoarding

"And He said unto them "Take care and be on your guard against all covetousness for one's life does not consist in the abundance of his possessions."

-    *Luke 12:15*

Day 1

Dear Lord, grant me the strength to recognize the signs of hoarding within myself and the courage to seek help.

Day 2

Heavenly Father, help me release my attachment to material possessions and find joy in simplicity.

Day 3

Lord, I pray for those who struggle with hoarding tendencies, that they may find peace and freedom from their burdens.

Day 4

God of mercy, grant me the wisdom to discern between what I need and what I simply want.

Day 5

Heavenly Father, help me to let go of my fear of scarcity and trust in your abundance.

Day 6

Lord, give me the grace to prioritize relationships over possessions and to cherish the moments spent with loved ones.

Day 7

Give me the humility to accept the assistance of others and the readiness to let go of what is redundant.

Day 8

Dear Lord Jesus, teach me to find contentment in your presence, not in anything else.

Day 9

Heal my wounds, God, which lead me into hoarding behavior and direct me toward emotional and spiritual health.

Day 10

Heavenly Father, help me find the strength to address the underlying issues driving my hoarding tendencies with honesty and courage.

Day 11

Help me, O God, to see the value of decluttering my life and the spaces around me.

Day 12

God, have mercy on me and help me by your grace to forgive past errors and omissions, so I do not emotionally hoard all things.

Day 13

Lord Jesus, shine your light into the darkness of my hoarding patterns and lead me towards freedom and redemption.

Day 14

Almighty Father, detach me from material things and help me find joy through serving others.

Day 15

Thank you for giving me the clarity to see that when I acquire things, I am using these things as a mask to try to cover my emotional needs.

Day 16

Dear Lord, give me the strength to let go of attachments to material things and embrace a life of simplicity and thankfulness.

Day 17

Dear God, give me the courage to seek professional help and support to overcome my hoarding tendencies.

Day 18

Assist me, Heavenly Father, to have a spirit of generosity and sharing, knowing that true abundance comes from giving.

Day 19

Lord Jesus, guide me to better ways of managing stress and anxiety instead of seeking refuge in possessions.

Day 20

God, grant me the serenity to let go of my attachment to material wealth and instead feel safe with you in your love and provision.

Day 21

Father God, help me realize the harm I am causing myself and others due to hoarding. Lord, give me the strength to break free from its hold.

Day 22

Dear Heavenly Father, make me humble to ask for help when I need it and brave to receive the help without shame.

Day 23

Lord Jesus, teach me how to appreciate the little joys and not to be on a continuous quest for more possessions.

Day 24

God, help me to easily differentiate what is of value to me and what is simply clutter in my life.

Day 25

Dear Lord, guide me to let go of my attachment to my possessions and to find joy in the freedom of a life clutter-free.

Day 26

Heavenly Father, give me the strength to face the emotions behind my hoarding behaviors and the courage to confront them honestly.

Day 27

Lord, help me to release the items and things that are from the past and to appreciate being in the moment, allowing openness and gratitude toward all that is in the present.

Day 28

God of mercy, grant me strength and continued patience to carry out the process of decluttering life, one thing at a time.

Day 29

Lord Jesus, in your great measure of love and compassion, may I be able to offer myself grace on this journey of healing and cleansing my life of excess.

Day 30

Heavenly Father, thank you for your constant presence and guidance in my life. Help me to trust in your provision and to find true fulfillment in you alone.

LESSONS FROM YOUR 30 DAY JOURNEY

(document your learnings from your 30 days of situational prayer)

Disloyalty

"For there is nothing hidden that will not be disclosed, and nothing concealed that will not be known or brought out into the open".

-      Luke 8:17

Day 1

Dear God, grant me the strength to forgive those who have been disloyal to me, and help me to release any bitterness or resentment from my heart.

Day 2

Heavenly Father, guide me in discerning true loyalty from falsehood and help me to surround myself with trustworthy individuals.

Day 3

Lord, protect me from the pain of disloyalty and grant me the wisdom to recognize signs of betrayal before they occur.

Day 4

God of mercy, heal the wounds caused by disloyalty and help me to find healing and restoration in your love.

Day 5

Lord Jesus, teach me to be a faithful and loyal friend, spouse, and companion, modeling your example of unconditional love and fidelity.

Day 6

Dear God, help me to be unwavering with you, even in times of temptation and challenge.

Day 7

Help me, Heavenly Father, to forgive myself for any times when I have failed others and guide me to make amends with them and seek reconciliation.

Day 8

Lord, help me to confront disloyalty with grace and dignity, to respond lovingly and not in vengeance.

Day 9

O God, protect my heart from the pain of betrayal and help me trust your faithfulness when everyone else lets me down.

Day 10

Lord Jesus, let me be surrounded by faithful and supportive relationships, and help me to be a loyal and trustworthy friend in return.

Day 11

Lord God, give me the courage to face the disloyalty;
direct me to confront it with love.

Day 12

God help me find healing from past betrayed trust and
move forward with confidence in your trustworthiness.

Day 13

O Lord. give me grace to forgive all who have betrayed
me, and let me release them into your hands for
judgment and redemption.

Day 14

Father, vindicate me in false accusations and slander,
and bring peace with your unfailing love.

Day 15

My Lord Jesus Christ, give me strength and
determination to be true to you and your words, even
when some have other thoughts.

Day 16

Give me wisdom, Lord, to see when loyalty will be served best by tough love, forgiveness, and reconciliation.

Day 17

Assist me, dear Lord, to be committed to the spirit of loyalty and devotion in all my relationships and faithful to my promises.

Day 18

Shield me, Lord, from all attempts of betrayal and temper me in every interaction that I may seek to establish a loyal friendship with others.

Day 19

God, grant me the courage to confront my own tendencies towards disloyalty, to seek your grace for forgiveness and redemption.

Day 20

Lord Jesus, surround me with true friends and loved ones and help me to be a faithful steward of their trust.

Day 21

Give me the grace, O Lord, to go through betrayals,
and may I find hope and healing within your promises.

Day 22

Lord, give me the grace to forgive whoever has been
disloyal to me and set them free from guilt.

Day 23

O Lord, let me look not at the hurt of unfaithfulness
but at the growth and change adversity brings.

Day 24

Lord of compassion, who consoles all my sorrows, give
me grace and strength to walk before you in dignity.

Day 25

Lord Jesus, hear my prayer to forgive myself for the
times I turned my back on you and others, and help
me allow you to order my steps.

Day 26

Heavenly Father, give me the wisdom to distinguish between trust and care and give me a spirit of discernment in all relationships.

Day 27

Dear God, save me from those who would influence me in the wrong direction and help me stand firm on the path to your truth.

Day 28

Lord, grant me the strength to speak the truth and be honest, even in the face of disloyalty, and find ways to bring reconciliation and peace, if possible.

Day 29

Grant me the grace, O God, to let go of past hurts and to embrace with confidence that you will heal all wounds.

Day 30

Enable me to trust in your promise to never leave me or forsake me, Lord Jesus, and to find my strength and comfort in your undergirding love.

LESSONS FROM YOUR 30 DAY JOURNEY

(document your learnings from your 30 days of situational prayer)

Shyness

"Who has made man's mouth? Who makes him mute, deaf, or seeing, or blind? Is it not I, the Lord? Now therefore go, and I will be with your mouth and teach you what you shall speak."

-Exodus 4:11-12

Day 1

Dear God, grant me the courage to overcome my shyness and to step out of my comfort zone with confidence.

Day 2

Heavenly Father, help me to see myself as you see me, with worth and value beyond my shyness.

Day 3

Lord, ease my anxiety and give me the strength to interact with others in a way that honors you.

Day 4

God of compassion, help me to be so passionate about your works that I am unable to keep a closed mouth.

Day 5

Lord Jesus, help me to take you into every conversation knowing that you will be my tongue.

Day 6

Dear God, grant me the courage to face my fears of rejection and judgment, knowing that you are always by my side.

Day 7

Heavenly Father, help me to find strength in my weaknesses and to see my shyness as an opportunity for growth and transformation.

Day 8

Lord, surround me with understanding and supportive people who can help me overcome my shyness with love and encouragement.

Day 9

God, grant me the confidence to share my thoughts and ideas with others, knowing that my voice is valuable and worthy of being heard.

Day 10

Lord Jesus, help me to overcome feelings of self-consciousness and insecurity, and to find freedom in expressing myself authentically.

Day 11

Dear God, grant me the grace to accept myself as I am, shyness and all, and to embrace the unique gifts and talents you have given me.

Day 12

Heavenly Father, help me to articulate your mighty works so that others can know you.

Day 13

Lord, guide me in developing healthy boundaries and assertiveness, so that I may navigate social situations with confidence and grace.

Day 14

God of courage, grant me the strength to face my fears and to step out in faith, knowing that you are with me every step of the way.

Day 15

Lord Jesus, help me to cultivate self-confidence and resilience, so that I may overcome my shyness and fulfill the purpose you have for my life.

Day 16

God grant me the serenity to accept the occasions when my shyness gets in my way and the courage to take little steps toward growth and change.

Day 17

Place me, Heavenly Father, in self-actualizing and self-discovering situations so that I can break from my shyness.

Day 18

Please make me see that my shyness is not a weakness but one of the unique ways you can make me an instrument for your glory.

Day 19

God, grant me the courage to leave the security of my comfort zone, knowing very well that you are there for me.

Day 20

Dearest Lord Jesus, help me to see your plans for my life; then, maybe I can overcome my shyness and live boldly for you.

Day 21

Dear God, help me to be kind and patient with myself in overcoming shyness, realizing it's the process of growth that calls for both time and labor.

Day 22

Divine Father, please help me to view shyness as an area in which I can spiritually grow and help me to rely on you for the strength and guidance to overcome shyness.

Day 23

Put my Lord, friends, and mentors by my side who may encourage and help me overcome shyness with love and understanding.

Day 24

God of courage, strengthen me so that I am more comfortable taking risks and moving forward toward opportunities that offer me growth and elevation.

Day 25

Help me find my voice, Lord Jesus, to speak, not just for me but for others, even when faced with fear and uncertainty.

Day 26

God, help me to believe in myself and chase my dreams and ambitions, with the understanding that you have given me all that is under the sun to succeed in my pursuits.

Day 27

Heavenly Father, help me to see my shyness not as an obstacle but as an opportunity to lean on your strength and grace as I step aside.

Day 28

Lord, give me the courage to take risks and lean on faith that you will supply all my needs.

Day 29

Help me to know how to be brave and courageous, dear God, to overcome shyness and fulfill all that you have called me to be.

Day 30

Jesus, thank you for such love over my life. Help me to trust your plan and to step into faith, being assured you will always be there.

LESSONS FROM YOUR 30 DAY JOURNEY

(document your learnings from your 30 days of situational prayer)

Excess

"Do not love the world or the things in the world. If anyone loves the world, the love of the Father is not in him. For all that is in the world, the desires of the flesh and the desires of the eyes and pride of life, is not from the Father, but is from the world. And the world is passing away along with its desires, but whoever does the will of God abides forever."

-     *1 John 2:15-17*

Day 1

Dear God, help me to recognize and acknowledge the areas of excess in my life, whether they be material possessions, indulgences, or unhealthy habits.

Day 2

Heavenly Father, grant me the wisdom to discern between genuine needs and unnecessary wants, and the strength to prioritize what truly matters.

Day 3

Lord, free me from the grip of consumption and the pursuit of excess and guide me towards a life of simplicity and contentment.

Day 4

God of moderation, help me to find balance in all aspects of my life, avoiding both excess and deprivation.

Day 5

Lord Jesus, teach me to steward my resources wisely, using them to bless others and glorify your name rather than indulging in extravagance for selfish gain.

Day 6

Father, give me the humility to realize when excess has been committed in words, thoughts, or desires, and the self-discipline to correct these things.

Day 7

God Almighty, help me to have a thankful heart for your blessings and help me to learn how to give liberally without wallowing in excess.

Day 8

Lord, grant me self-discipline that I may not fall for temptations of excess but live a life of moderation and temperance.

Day 9

God, reveal in my life everything that comes from spiritual increase and intimacy with you. Give me the grace and strength to let go of things that are not your will.

Day 10

God, freeze the part of my heart that always yearns for more and more things to make me happy.

Day 11

Dear Lord, grant me strength to resist the cultural pressures and norms of society, which press humans into excess and over-indulgence, and enable me to live counter-culturally standing on your word.

Day 12

Dear Heavenly Father, please guide me to healthy boundaries and priorities so that a balanced and meaningful life can be conducted free from the yokes of excess.

Day 13

Let me release the fear of scarcity, Lord, that drives me to seek my security in excess, for I will trust in your provision and abundance.

Day 14

Grace-filled and merciful God, forgive me for the times I have squandered your blessings with extravagance and wastefulness. Teach me to be wise and responsible.

Day 15

Lord Jesus, give me the courage to break out of the vicious cycle of endless consumption and excess and find true fulfillment in living by your will.

Day 16

Dear God, open my eyes to how excess bars me from receiving all you offer in life and that by trusting in you all things will be provided.

Day 17

Father in Heaven, show me what causes hurt to my body, soul, and spirit; let me follow the alternative path of moderation and self-care.

Day 18

Help me, Lord, to resist instant gratification and the lure of earthly things, knowing that my treasures are stored in Heaven.

Day 19

God, help me to use what you have given me—my resources, time, and talents—in a way that honors you and blesses others, and not in such a way that I just squander them on purely selfish pursuits of excess.

Day 20

Lord Jesus, teach me to find my satisfaction and contentment in thee alone rather than in any heap of possessions, wealth, or experiences.

Day 21

Grant me, Lord, the humility to recognize when I have been excessive in my desires, actions, or attitudes and the grace to repent and turn to a more balanced and righteous way of living.

Day 22

Dear God, help me be strong enough to live open-handed, able to give and receive according to your will, and not to be ensnared by clinging to possessions or pursuing wealth over and above measure.

Day 23

Almighty God, rescue me from greed, selfishness, and materialism; grant me a heart of generosity, gratitude, and contentment.

Day 24

Provide for my needs, O Lord, and help me be content with what is given to me, not always striving for more out of fear of lack.

Day 25

Lord Jesus, give me the courage to turn and face the false gods of plenty that have become part of my life, and the strength to rebuke them and look toward Heaven.

Day 26

Help me, God, to consider myself responsible for how I use the resources you have provided me, and be a godly steward who uses them for your glory.

Day 27

Heavenly Father, grant me the discernment to recognize when I am being driven by the spirit of excess rather than led by your Holy Spirit, and the humility to submit to your will.

Day 28

Lord, help me to find balance and moderation in all areas of my life, whether it be in my consumption of food and drink, my use of time and money, or my pursuit of pleasure and entertainment.

Day 29

Father God, help me not to be overcome by the desire to impress others with worldly things but show them the God in me and your mighty works.

Day 30

Lord Jesus, thank you for your grace and mercy, which cover my failures and shortcomings. Help me to live in the freedom and abundance that comes from surrendering to your will and trusting in your provision.

LESSONS FROM YOUR 30 DAY JOURNEY

(document your learnings from your 30 days of situational prayer)

Money

"Do not toil to acquire wealth; be discerning enough to desist (refrain). When your eyes light on it, it is gone, for suddenly it sprouts wings, flying like an eagle toward heaven."

-     Proverbs 23:4-5

Day 1

Dear God, grant me the wisdom to manage my finances wisely, honoring you with the resources you have entrusted to me.

Day 2

Heavenly Father, help me to view money as a tool for good, to be used for the betterment of others and the advancement of your kingdom.

Day 3

Lord, help me make sound judgments concerning my finances in ways that align with your will and bring glory to your name.

Day 4

Give me, O God, the power to avoid the temptations of greed and selfishness and the virtue to be found worthy of sharing my blessings with others.

Day 5

Help me, Jesus, that I learn to be content in you, not in material possessions, and to rely on your provision regarding all my needs.

Day 6

God, bestow on me a grateful frame of mind for the bounty in my life. May you give me the humility to see your hand in each blessing of financial abundance.

Day 7

Almighty Father, guard me against the love of money, which may lead to all kinds of evil, and help me keep my priorities on track with your kingdom's purpose.

Day 8

Lord, help me realize that if I am faithful over a few things, you will make me master of much.

Day 9

God, help me be good and wise in managing the resources you have provided for your glory.

Day 10

Lord Jesus, help me to overcome my fears and anxieties about money and to trust in your faithfulness and provision in all circumstances.

Day 11

Grant me this grace, dear God: be content with what I have rather than always striving to have more wealth and possessions.

Day 12

Allow me, O Heavenly Father, to be closer to your acceptable standards concerning money—never holding it or wasting it but using it wisely and generously for the sake of your kingdom.

Day 13

Deliver me, O Lord, from the slippery walk of debt and financial bondage; help me to live within my means and to be a good steward of the resources You have provided.

Day 14

God, give me discernment to resist where worldly desires lead and give me the power to always rebuke materialism and greed.

Day 15

Lord Jesus, grant that I may be generous and cheerful in giving, knowing that you love a cheerful giver and will bless those who give with a joyful heart.

Day 16

Give me humility that I may seek wise guidance and advice in my financial decisions and give me the courage to follow that guidance when it may be contrary to popular advice.

Day 17

Heavenly Father, help me to understand that wealth is not only measured by money, but one can be rich in health and love.

Day 18

Lord, grant me the wisdom to save and invest wisely for the future, trusting in your provision and guidance every step of the way.

Day 19

God, help me to cultivate a spirit of generosity and abundance, knowing that as I give, so shall I receive, pressed down, shaken together, and running over.

Day 20

Lord Jesus, teach me to be content with having "enough" rather than always striving for "more," and to find true fulfillment in serving you rather than in accumulating wealth.

Day 21

Dear God, grant me the strength to resist the pressures of our consumer culture and to live simply and modestly, according to your teachings.

Day 22

Heavenly Father, help me to not rob you of the resources that are due unto you, knowing that you will rebuke the devourer of my finances.

Day 23

Lord, protect me from the love of money, which can lead to greed, envy, and discontentment, and help me to find true riches in you alone.

Day 24

God, grant me the ability to hear your voice when dealing with financial matters and not be driven by greed in my decision-making.

Day 25

Lord Jesus, guide me to be aware of others' needs and to use my financial resources to ease suffering and promote kindness in the world.

Day 26

Dear God, give me the humility to recognize that everything I have is yours, and the willingness to use it in ways that honor and glorify your name.

Day 27

Heavenly Father, help me to be a responsible steward of the earth's resources, using them wisely and responsibly for the benefit of current and future generations.

Day 28

Lord, grant me the wisdom to prioritize my spending according to your values and principles, rather than the fleeting desires of this world.

Day 29

God, help me to be generous in sharing my financial blessings with others, knowing that as I give, so shall I receive, abundantly and overflowing.

Day 30

Lord Jesus, thank you for the many blessings you have bestowed upon me, including the gift of financial abundance. Help me to use these blessings wisely and generously for your glory and the advancement of your kingdom.

LESSONS FROM YOUR 30 DAY JOURNEY

(document your learnings from your 30 days of situational prayer)

Health

"Or do you not know that your body is a temple of the Holy Spirit within you, whom you have from God? You are not your own."

- *1 Corinthians 6:19*

Day 1

Dear God, I pray for physical strength and vitality to carry out your will and serve others with love and compassion.

Day 2

Heavenly Father, grant me the wisdom to make healthy choices that nourish my body, mind, and spirit.

Day 3

Lord, I pray for healing and restoration for those who are suffering from illness or injury, that they may experience your comforting presence and miraculous touch.

Day 4

God of mercy, I lift up those struggling with chronic conditions or disabilities, asking for your grace to sustain them and your power to bring about healing according to your will.

Day 5

Lord Jesus, I pray for mental and emotional well-being, that you would bring peace and clarity to troubled minds and hearts.

Day 6

Dear God, I ask for protection from illness and disease, and for strength to endure times of sickness with faith and patience.

Day 7

Heavenly Father, I pray for healthcare workers and caregivers, that you would grant them wisdom, compassion, and strength as they minister to the sick and suffering.

Day 8

Lord, I lift up those who are facing surgery or medical procedures, asking for your guiding hand to be upon the doctors and nurses, and for a successful outcome according to your divine plan.

Day 9

God, I pray for those struggling with addiction or substance abuse. Break their chains of bondage and bring freedom and wholeness to their lives.

Day 10

Lord Jesus, I lift up those battling mental illness. Please touch them with your healing power and grant them the support and understanding of family, friends, and community.

Day 11

Dear God, I ask for your protection and provision for the elderly and vulnerable. May they experience dignity, care, and love in their later years.

Day 12

Heavenly Father, I pray for those facing infertility or reproductive health challenges, asking for comfort, guidance, and the miracle of new life according to your perfect timing.

Day 13

Lord, I lift up those struggling with eating disorders or body image issues, asking for healing and restoration of self-worth and identity in you.

Day 14

God of hope, I pray for those dealing with chronic pain or disability, asking for relief, strength, and perseverance to face each day with courage and faith.

Day 15

Lord Jesus, I pray that you keep my mind and body strong, particularly as I progress in age.

Day 16

Dear God, I ask for your protection from accidents, injuries, and disasters, and for the courage and resilience to overcome adversity and rebuild anything that has been lost.

Day 17

Heavenly Father, I pray for the health and well-being of children and youth, asking for protection from harm and for opportunities to grow and thrive in body, mind, and spirit.

Day 18

Lord, I lift up those struggling with sleep disorders or insomnia, asking for restful sleep and rejuvenation for body, mind, and soul.

Day 19

God, I pray for those battling cancer or other life-threatening illnesses, asking for strength, courage, and faith to face each day with hope and trust in your healing power.

Day 20

Lord Jesus, I ask that you put your healing hands on those dealing with terminal illnesses and help them to know you have the power to change anything and everything.

Day 21

Dear God, I ask for your guidance and wisdom in caring for my body as your temple, making healthy choices, and practicing self-care to honor you and serve others more effectively.

Day 22

Heavenly Father, I pray for those struggling with a disability and that you will give them the strength to forge ahead knowing that where they are weak, you will make them strong.

Day 23

Lord, I ask that you console those caring for ill loved ones and that you give them the strength they need to provide quality care.

Day 24

God of comfort, I pray for those grieving the loss of loved ones, asking for your presence to surround them with peace, hope, and the assurance of eternal life.

Day 25

Lord Jesus, I pray for those struggling with addictions or destructive behaviors, asking for freedom, deliverance, and transformation by the power of your Holy Spirit.

Day 26

Dear God, I ask for your protection and healing for those living in areas affected by natural disasters, epidemics, or humanitarian crises, that they may find strength and resilience in the midst of adversity.

Day 27

Heavenly Father, I pray for those facing financial hardship or insecurity. Please provide guidance and opportunities to help them overcome obstacles and build a brighter future.

Day 28

Lord, I ask for your protection for the unhoused. Keep their bodies healthy as they endure the elements and navigate the challenges of homelessness.

Day 29

God of grace, I pray for women struggling with physical ailments affecting their reproductive health. Place your healing hand on their wombs and cure them.

Day 30

Lord Jesus, I pray for the health and well-being of all your children. Touch them with your healing power and shower them with abundant blessings.

LESSONS FROM YOUR 30 DAY JOURNEY

(document your learnings from your 30 days of situational prayer)

Forgiveness

"Then Peter came up and said to him. "Lord how often will my brother sin against me and I forgive him? As many as seven times?" Jesus said to him, "I do not say to you seven times, but seventy-seven times."

-Matthew 18:21-22

Day 1

Dear God, grant me the strength to forgive those who have wronged me, just as you have forgiven me.

Day 2

Father, help me release the burden of resentment and anger, and embrace the freedom that comes from forgiveness.

Day 3

Lord, give me the grace to forgive myself for past mistakes and shortcomings, and to move forward with humility and compassion.

Day 4

God of mercy, grant me the courage to seek forgiveness from those I have hurt, and the humility to make amends and seek reconciliation.

Day 5

Lord Jesus, guide me to love my enemies and pray for those who've wronged me. Let me find peace and healing through forgiveness.

Day 6

Dear God, help me release grudges and bitterness. Teach me to offer grace and forgiveness even to those who may not seem to deserve it.

Day 7

Heavenly Father, give me the wisdom to look beyond others' flaws and see their inherent worth and dignity as your child.

Day 8

Lord, I seek the strength to forgive even when it feels impossible. Let your grace soften my heart and heal my wounds.

Day 9

God, remind me that forgiveness is not about condoning wrongs but about freeing my heart from the grip of hurt and resentment.

Day 10

Lord Jesus, may your example of forgiveness on the cross inspire me, where you prayed, "Father, forgive them, for they know not what they do."

Day 11

Dear God, grant me the humility to recognize my need for forgiveness and the willingness to extend it to others.

Day 12

Heavenly Father, help me view forgiveness as a strength and embrace the healing that comes with letting go of past hurts.

Day 13

Lord, I pray for the courage to face the pain of betrayal and choose forgiveness as a path to wholeness and reconciliation.

Day 14

God of grace, give me the patience to forgive others, even when they do not acknowledge or repent for their actions.

Day 15

Lord Jesus, help me forgive those who have deeply hurt me, understanding that in forgiving them, I free myself from resentment and bitterness.

Day 16

Dear God, remind us that you are a God of second chances, and we should extend the same grace to others.

Day 17

Heavenly Father, help me forgive those who have repeatedly hurt me, breaking the cycle of resentment and retaliation with love and compassion.

Day 18

Lord, grant me the courage and strength to approach those who have wronged me with forgiveness and love.

Day 19

God of mercy, help me release the burden of past hurts and embrace a future filled with hope, joy, and peace.

Day 20

Lord Jesus, teach me to forgive as you have forgiven me, with grace, compassion, and overflowing love.

Day 21

Dear God, help me let go of the need for revenge or retribution and choose forgiveness as a path to healing and reconciliation.

Day 22

Heavenly Father, grant me the wisdom to see forgiveness as an ongoing process, and the perseverance to continue extending grace and compassion to others.

Day 23

Lord, I pray for the courage to forgive those who have betrayed my trust, and rebuild relationships based on honesty, transparency, and forgiveness.

Day 24

God of grace, grant me the humility to accept forgiveness from others with gratitude, and the willingness to learn and grow from my mistakes.

Day 25

Lord Jesus, help me forgive those who have hurt me deeply, and release them into your hands, trusting your justice and mercy to heal and restore all things.

Day 26

Dear God, help me understand that being the first to apologize is not a sign of weakness, but an act of freeing myself from hate and resentment.

Day 27

Heavenly Father, help me to extend forgiveness even when it feels undeserved or difficult, knowing that in doing so, I reflect your grace and mercy to the world.

Day 28

Lord, I pray for the grace to forgive those who have hurt me, and to release them from the hold they have on my heart, trusting in your love and sovereignty to bring healing and redemption.

Day 29

God of compassion, as you grant us new mercies every day, help me model those same behaviors.

Day 30

Lord Jesus, thank you for the gift of forgiveness and the freedom it brings. Help me to extend that same forgiveness to others, knowing that in doing so, I participate in your redemptive work in the world.

LESSONS FROM YOUR 30 DAY JOURNEY

(document your learnings from your 30 days of situational prayer)

Faithfulness

> *"Let love and faithfulness never leave you; bind them around your neck, write them on the tablet of your heart."*
>
> -Proverbs 3:3-4

Day 1

Dear God, give me the strength to stay faithful to you, even in times of doubt and uncertainty.

Day 2

Heavenly Father, help me trust in your faithfulness, knowing you always keep your promises.

Day 3

Lord, grant me the grace to be faithful in my relationships, honoring my commitments, and treating others with love and respect.

Day 4

God of mercy, help me stay true to your teachings and commandments, striving to live a life that pleases you.

Day 5

Lord Jesus, teach me to be faithful in prayer, trusting in your power and provision to meet all my needs.

Day 6

Dear God, give me the courage to stand firm in my faith, even when faced with opposition or persecution.

Day 7

Heavenly Father, help me be faithful in using the gifts and talents you've given me to serve others and glorify your name.

Day 8

Lord, I pray for the strength to resist temptation and stay true to your word, even when it goes against the ways of the world.

Day 9

God, help me be faithful in my worship and devotion, setting aside time each day to seek your presence and draw closer to you.

Day 10

Lord Jesus, grant me the grace to be faithful in obeying your will, trusting that your ways are higher than mine.

Day 11

Dear God, give me the humility to acknowledge my shortcomings and the grace to repent and turn back to you in faithfulness.

Day 12

Heavenly Father, help me be faithful in serving others, following the example of Jesus who came to serve, not to be served.

Day 13

Lord, grant me the courage to step out in faith and trust you to lead me, even when the path ahead is uncertain.

Day 14

God of grace, help me be faithful in forgiveness, extending mercy and grace to others as you have shown to me.

Day 15

Lord Jesus, you promised never to leave me nor forsake me; help me see your faithfulness in my life.

Day 16

Dear God, grant me the wisdom to discern your will and the courage to follow where you lead, trusting in your faithfulness to guide me.

Day 17

Heavenly Father, help me be faithful in my words and actions, letting my light shine before others so they may see your goodness and glorify you.

Day 18

Lord, give me the grace to remain faithful during times of testing and trial, knowing you are with me and will never leave me.

Day 19

God, help me be faithful in giving, sharing generously with others, and trusting in your provision for all my needs.

Day 20

Lord Jesus, grant me the courage to stand up for what is right and just, even when it is unpopular or difficult.

Day 21

Dear God, give me the strength to endure hardships and suffering with faithfulness, knowing you are working all things together for my good.

Day 22

Heavenly Father, help me be faithful in what you have called me to do, trusting that you will grant me great favor if I do.

Day 23

Lord, give me the grace to be faithful in my commitments and responsibilities, honoring my word and fulfilling my obligations.

Day 24

God of hope, help me be faithful in waiting, trusting in your timing, and believing that you will fulfill your promises in due season.

Day 25

Lord Jesus, I pray for the courage to share my faith with others, boldly proclaiming the good news of your love and salvation.

Day 26

Dear God, grant me the humility to admit when I have been unfaithful and the grace to seek forgiveness and restoration.

Day 27

Heavenly Father, help me to be faithful in my thoughts and attitudes, renewing my mind daily with your word, and seeking to align my heart with your will.

Day 28

Lord, help me to be faithful in my prayer life knowing that prayer is powerful and changes things.

Day 29

God, help me to be faithful in my worship and praise, lifting my voice in adoration and thanksgiving for all your goodness and mercy.

Day 30

Lord Jesus, thank you for your faithfulness to me. Help me to walk in faithfulness and obedience all the days of my life, that I may bring glory and honor to your name.

LESSONS FROM YOUR 30 DAY JOURNEY

(document your learnings from your 30 days of situational prayer)

This book is dedicated to the Glory of God and the memory of my beloved parents, ***Jesse*** and ***Clarkye Wilks.***